The Blackbird in the Lilac

POEMS FOR CHILDREN

The Blackbird in the Lilac

JAMES REEVES

Illustrated by
EDWARD ARDIZZONE

London
OXFORD UNIVERSITY PRESS

Oxford University Press, Ely House, London W. 1

GLASGOW NEW YORK TORONTO MELBOURNE WELLINGTON
CAPE TOWN IBADAN NAIROBI DAR ES SALAAM LUSAKA ADDIS ABABA
DELHI BOMBAY CALCUTTA MADRAS KARACHI LAHORE DACCA
KUALA LUMPUR SINGAPORE HONG KONG TOKYO

ISBN 0 19 276005 X

First published 1952
Reprinted 1957, 1962, 1967, 1972

PRINTED IN GREAT BRITAIN

To
GARETH

James Reeves has also written

THE WANDERING MOON
poems for children
(*Messrs. William Heinemann*)

The poem *Yellow Wheels* first
appeared in a collection of poems
for small children published
by Messrs. William Heinemann
under that name

Contents

THE BLACKBIRD

IN THE LILAC

The Blackbird in the Lilac

'Good fortune!' and 'Good fortune!'
I heard the blackbird in the lilac say,
As I set out upon the road to somewhere,
   That sunny summer's day.

  Gay ribbons and sad ballads
And suchlike things I carried in my pack,
But thought of home was heavier than the load
   I had upon my back.

  'Come buy, come buy, fine people!'
I cried on bridges and in market squares;
On village greens I showed my toys and trifles,
   But none would have my wares.

  Yet still I sing my ballads,
And think of home, and go where fortune leads.
Homewards I will not turn without good fortune,
   Though none my singing heeds.

  For still I hear the blackbird
Wish me good fortune from the lilac sweet:
Such songs as his, amid the summer's promise,
   Could never be deceit.

DANCE

AND RHYME

Yellow Wheels

A yellow gig has Farmer Patch;
   He drives a handsome mare—
Two bright wheels and four bright hooves
   To carry him to the fair.

   Yellow wheels, where are you off to,
      Twinkling down the lane,
   Sparkling in the April sunshine
      And the April rain?

Farmer Patch we do not love;
   He wears a crusty frown.
But how we love to see his gig
   Go spanking off to town!

Yellow wheels, where are you off to,
Twinkling down the lane,
Sparkling in the April sunshine
And the April rain?

Run a Little

Run a little this way,
    Run a little that!
Fine new feathers
    For a fine new hat.
A fine new hat
    For a lady fair—
Run around and turn about
    And jump in the air.

Run a little this way,
    Run a little that!
White silk ribbon
    For a black silk cat.
A black silk cat
    For the Lord Mayor's wife—
Run around and turn about
    And fly for your life!

The Two Mice

There met two mice at Scarborough
    Beside the rushing sea,
The one from Market Harborough,
    The other from Dundee.

They shook their feet, they clapped their hands,
    And twirled their tails about;
They danced all day upon the sands
    Until the stars peeped out.

'I'm much fatigued,' the one mouse sighed,
    'And ready for my tea.'
'Come hame awa',' the other cried,
    'And tak' a crumb wi' me.'

They slept awhile, and then next day
    Across the moors they went;
But sad to say, they lost their way
    And came to Stoke-on-Trent.

And there it soon began to rain,
  At which they cried full sore:
'If ever we get home again,
  We'll not go dancing more.'

If Pigs Could Fly

If pigs could fly, I'd fly a pig
To foreign countries small and big—
      To Italy and Spain,
To Austria, where cowbells ring,
To Germany, where people sing—
      And then come home again.

I'd see the Ganges and the Nile;
I'd visit Madagascar's isle,
      And Persia and Peru.
People would say they'd never seen
So odd, so strange an air-machine
      As that on which I flew.

Why, everyone would raise a shout
To see his trotters and his snout
      Come floating from the sky;
And I would be a famous star
Well known in countries near and far—
      If only pigs could fly!

Mick

Mick my mongrel-O
   Lives in a bungalow,
Painted green with a round doorway.
   With an eye for cats
   And a nose for rats
He lies on his threshold half the day.
   He buries his bones
   By the rockery stones,
And never, oh never, forgets the place.
   Ragged and thin
   From his tail to his chin,
He looks at you with a sideways face.
   Dusty and brownish,
   Wicked and clownish,
He'll win no prize at the County Show.
   But throw him a stick,
   And up jumps Mick,
And right through the flower-beds see him go!

The Old Wife and the Ghost

There was an old wife and she lived all alone
  In a cottage not far from Hitchin:
And one bright night, by the full moon light,
  Comes a ghost right into her kitchen.

About that kitchen neat and clean
  The ghost goes pottering round.
But the poor old wife is deaf as a boot
  And so hears never a sound.

The ghost blows up the kitchen fire,
  As bold as bold can be;
He helps himself from the larder shelf,
  But never a sound hears she.

He blows on his hands to make them warm,
  And whistles aloud 'Whee-hee!'
But still as a sack the old soul lies
  And never a sound hears she.

From corner to corner he runs about,
  And into the cupboard he peeps;
He rattles the door and bumps on the floor,
  But still the old wife sleeps.

Jangle and bang go the pots and pans,
  As he throws them all around;
And the plates and mugs and dishes and jugs,
  He flings them all to the ground.

Madly the ghost tears up and down
  And screams like a storm at sea;
And at last the old wife stirs in her bed—
  And it's 'Drat those mice,' says she.

Then the first cock crows and morning shows
  And the troublesome ghost's away.
But oh! what a pickle the poor wife sees
  When she gets up next day.

'Them's tidy big mice,' the old wife thinks,
  And off she goes to Hitchin,
And a tidy big cat she fetches back
  To keep the mice from her kitchen.

W

The King sent for his wise men all
    To find a rhyme for W;
When they had thought a good long time
But could not think of a single rhyme,
    'I'm sorry,' said he, 'to trouble you.'

A Pig Tale

Poor Jane Higgins,
　She had five piggins,
And one got drowned in the Irish Sea.
　Poor Jane Higgins,
　She had four piggins,
And one flew over a sycamore tree.
　Poor Jane Higgins,
　She had three piggins,
And one was taken away for pork.
　Poor Jane Higgins,
　She had two piggins,
And one was sent to the Bishop of Cork.
　Poor Jane Higgins,
　She had one piggin,
And that was struck by a shower of hail,
　So poor Jane Higgins,
　She had no piggins,
And that's the end of my little pig tale.

The Three Unlucky Men

Near Wookey Hole in days gone by
    Lived three unlucky men.
The first fell down a Treacle Mine
    And never stirred again.

The second had no better fate
    And he too is no more.
He fell into a Custard Lake
    And could not get to shore.

The third poor fellow, sad to say,
    He had no fairer luck,
For he climbed up a Porridge Hill
    And half-way down got stuck.

Alas, alas! man is but grass,
　　Let life be short or long;
And all the birds cried 'Fancy that!'
　　To hear this merry song.

The Footprint

Poor Crusoe saw with fear-struck eyes
    The footprint on the shore—
Oh! what is this that shines so clear
    Upon the bathroom floor?

The Four Letters

N,
  S,
    W,
      and E—
These are the letters which I can see
High on top of the old grey church
Where the golden rooster has his perch.
What they mean I do not know,
Though somebody told me long ago.
It might be that and it might be this,
But here is what I *think* it is:
N for Nowhere, S for Somewhere,
E for Everywhere, and W for Where—
And if I am wrong, I don't much care.

The Ceremonial Band

(To be said out loud by a chorus and solo voices)

The old King of Dorchester,
He had a little orchestra,
And never did you hear such a ceremonial band.
'Tootle-too,' said the flute,
'Deed-a-reedle,' said the fiddle,
For the fiddles and the flutes were the finest in the land.

The old King of Dorchester,
He had a little orchestra,
And never did you hear such a ceremonial band.
'Pump-a-rum,' said the drum,
'Tootle-too,' said the flute,
'Deed-a-reedle,' said the fiddle,
For the fiddles and the flutes were the finest in the land.

The old King of Dorchester,
He had a little orchestra,
And never did you hear such a ceremonial band.
'Pickle-pee,' said the fife,
'Pump-a-rum,' said the drum,
'Tootle-too,' said the flute,
'Deed-a-reedle,' said the fiddle,
For the fiddles and the flutes were the finest in the land.

The old King of Dorchester,
He had a little orchestra,
And never did you hear such a ceremonial band.
'Zoomba-zoom', said the bass,
'Pickle-pee,' said the fife,
'Pump-a-rum,' said the drum,
'Tootle-too,' said the flute,
'Deed-a-reedle,' said the fiddle,
For the fiddles and the flutes were the finest in the land.

The old King of Dorchester,
He had a little orchestra,
And never did you hear such a ceremonial band.
'Pah-pa-rah,' said the trumpet,
'Zoomba-zoom,' said the bass,
'Pickle-pee,' said the fife,
'Pump-a-rum,' said the drum,
'Tootle-too,' said the flute,
'Deed-a-reedle,' said the fiddle,
For the fiddles and the flutes were the finest in the land,
Oh! the fiddles and the flutes were the finest in the land!

HEDGE

AND HARVEST

Explorers

The furry moth explores the night,
    The fish discover cities drowned,
And moles and worms and ants explore
    The many cupboards underground.

The soaring lark explores the sky,
    And gulls explore the stormy seas.
The busy squirrel rummages
    Among the attics of the trees.

Bluebells and Foxgloves

If bluebells could be rung
    In early summer time,
The sound you'd hear would be
    A small, silvery chime.

The bells on foxglove spires,
    If they could once be tolled,
Would give a mellow sound
    As deep and rich as gold.

The bluebells and foxgloves—
    If they together pealed,
Who knows what elfin footsteps
    Would crowd across the field?

The Intruder

Two-boots in the forest walks,
Pushing through the bracken stalks.

Vanishing like a puff of smoke,
Nimbletail flies up the oak.

Longears helter-skelter shoots
Into his house among the roots.

At work upon the highest bark,
Tapperbill knocks off to hark.

Painted-wings through sun and shade
Flounces off along the glade.

Not a creature lingers by,
When clumping Two-boots comes to pry.

The Grasshopper and the Bird

The grasshopper said
To the bird in the tree
  Zik-a-zik zik-a-zik
As polite as could be—
  Zik-a-zik zik-a-zik—
Which he meant for to say
In his grasshopper way
For the time of the year
'Twas a *vairy* warm day—
  Zik-a-zik zik-a-zik—
What a very warm day!

  Tee-oo-ee tee-oo-ee
Said the bird in the tree,
  Tee-oo-ee tee-oo-ee
As polite as could be;
That's as much as to say—
  Tee-oo-ee tee-oo-ee
That I can't quite agree!
So he upped with his wings—
  Tee-oo-ee tee-oo-ee
And he flew from the tree.

So the grasshopper hopped
Four hops and away
  Snick!
    Click!
      Flick!
        Slick!—
Four hops and away
To the edge of the hay
  Zik-a-zik zik-a-zik
For the rest of the day.

Zik-a-zik zik-a-zik
Tee-oo-ee tee-oo-ee
The bird and the grasshopper
Can't quite agree.

Things to Remember

The buttercups in May,
The wild rose on the spray,
The poppy in the hay,

The primrose in the dell,
The freckled foxglove bell,
The honeysuckle's smell

Are things I would remember
When cheerless, raw November
Makes room for dark December.

Seeds

A row of pearls
Delicate green
Cased in white velvet—
The broad bean.

Smallest of birds
Winged and brown,
Seed of the maple
Flutters down.

Cupped like an egg
Without a yolk,
Grows the acorn,
Seed of the oak.

Autumn the housewife
Now unlocks
Seeds of the poppy
In their spice-box.

Silver hair
From an old man's crown
Wind-stolen
Is thistledown.

A Garden at Night

On powdery wings the white moths pass,
And petals fall on the dewy grass;
Over the bed where the poppy sleeps
The furtive fragrance of lavender creeps.
Here lived an old lady in days long gone,
And the ghost of that lady lingers on.
She sniffs the roses, and seems to see
The ripening fruit on the orchard tree;
Like the scent of flowers her spirit weaves
Its winding way through the maze of leaves;
Up and down like the moths it goes:
Never and never it finds repose.

Gentle she was, and quiet and kind,
But flitting and restless was her old mind.
So hither and thither across the lawn
Her spirit wanders, till grey of dawn
Rouses the cock in the valley far,
And the garden waits for the morning star.

Birds in the Forest

Birds in the forest sing
   Of meadows green;
They sing of primrose banks
   With pools between.

Birds in the forest sing
   Of gardens bright;
They sing of scented flowers
   That haunt the night.

Birds in the forest sing
   Of falling water,
Falling like the hair
   Of a king's daughter.

Birds in the forest sing
   Of foreign lands;
They sing of hills beyond
   The foamy sands.

They sing of a far mountain
   Topped by a town
Where sits a grey wizard
   In a gold crown.

The songs the wild birds sing
   In forests tall,
It was the old grey wizard
   Taught them all.

The Toadstool Wood

The toadstool wood is dark and mouldy,
  And has a ferny smell.
About the trees hangs something quiet
  And queer—like a spell.

Beneath the arching sprays of bramble
  Small creatures make their holes;
Over the moss's close green velvet
  The stilted spider strolls.

The stalks of toadstools pale and slender
  That grow from that old log,
Bars they might be to imprison
  A prince turned to a frog.

There lives no mumbling witch nor wizard
  In this uncanny place,
Yet you might think you saw at twilight
  A little, crafty face.

Cows

Half the time they munched the grass, and all the
   time they lay
Down in the water-meadows, the lazy month of May,
      A-chewing,
      A-mooing,
   To pass the hours away.

     'Nice weather,' said the brown cow.
      'Ah,' said the white.
    'Grass is very tasty.'
      'Grass is all right.'

Half the time they munched the grass, and all the
  time they lay
Down in the water-meadows, the lazy month of May,
          A-chewing,
          A-mooing,
     To pass the hours away.

          'Rain coming,' said the brown cow.
          'Ah,' said the white.
          'Flies is very tiresome.'
          'Flies bite.'

Half the time they munched the grass, and all the
  time they lay
Down in the water-meadows, the lazy month of May,
          A-chewing,
          A-mooing,
     To pass the hours away.

          'Time to go,' said the brown cow.
          'Ah', said the white.
          'Nice chat'. 'Very pleasant.'
          'Night.' 'Night.'

Half the time they munched the grass, and all the
  time they lay
Down in the water-meadows, the lazy month of May,
          A-chewing,
          A-mooing,
     To pass the hours away.

ELM TREES AND

OTHER PEOPLE

Trees in the Moonlight

Trees in the moonlight stand
    Still as a steeple,
And so quiet they seem like ghosts
    Of country people—

Dead farmers and their wives
    Of long, long ago,
Haunting the countryside
    They used to know;

Old gossips and talkers
    With tongues gone still;
Ploughmen rooted in the land
    They used to till;

Old carters and harvesters,
    Their wheels long rotten;
Old maids whose very names
    Time has forgotten.

Ghosts are they hereabouts;
    Them the moon sees,
Dark and still in the fields
    Like sleeping trees.

Long nights in autumn
    Hear them strain and cry,
Torn with a wordless sorrow
    As the gale sweeps by.

Spring makes fresh buds appear
    On the old boughs,
As if it could to their old wishes
    These ghosts arouse.

Trees in the summer night
    By moonlight linger on
So quiet they seem like ghosts
    Of people gone,

And it would be small wonder
    If at break of day
They heard the far-off cock-crow
    And fled away.

The Fiddler

The blind man lifts his violin
And tucks it up right under his chin;
He saws with his fiddle-stick to and fro
And out comes the music sorrowful slow.

Oh Shenandoah, it seems to say,
   Good-bye, you rolling river;
To Londonderry I'm away
   Beside the weeping willow.

Ha'pennies and pennies he gets but few
As he fiddles his old tunes through and through;
But he nods and smiles as he scrapes away
And out comes the music sprightly and gay.

To the Irish washerwoman dancing a jig
   In the land of Sweet Forever
Over the hills goes Tom with his pig,
   And it's there we'll surely follow!

Miss Wing

At the end of the street lives small Miss Wing,
A feathery, fluttery bird of a thing.
If you climb the street to the very top,
There you will see her fancy shop
With ribbons and buttons and frills and fluffs,
Pins and needles, purses and puffs,
Cosies and cushions and bits of chiffon,
And tiny hankies for ladies to sniff on,
And twists of silk and pieces of lace,
And odds and ends all over the place.
You push the door and the door-bell rings,
And the voice you hear is little Miss Wing's.
'Good-day, my dear, and how do you do?
Now tell me, what can I do for you?
Just half a second, please, dear Miss Gay—
As I was saying the other day—
Now what did I do with that so-and-so?
I'm sure I had it a moment ago—
As I was saying—why, yes, my dear—
A very nice day for the time of year—
Have you heard how poor Mrs. Such-and-such?—
Oh, I hope I haven't charged too much;
That would never do—Now, what about pink?
It's nice for children, I always think—
Some buttons to go with a lavender frock?
Why now, I believe I'm out of stock—
Well, what about these? Oh, I never knew—
I'm ever so sorry—now what about blue?
Such a very nice woman—a flower for a hat?'

And so she goes on, with 'Fancy that!'
And 'You never can tell,' and 'Oh dear, no,'
And 'There now! it only goes to show.'
And on she goes like a hank of tape,
A reel of ribbon, a roll of crêpe,
Till you think her tongue will never stop.

And that's Miss Wing of the fancy shop.

Mr. Bellairs

In a huge hoary mansion
　　Lives Mr. Bellairs,
With four or five stories
　　And hundreds of stairs.

The gates of his garden
　　Are made of wrought iron,
From the top of each gatepost
　　Glares down a great lion.

The trees in the garden
　　Are ancient and stately,
And high in their branches
　　Rooks mumble sedately.

The tails of the peacocks
　　Sweep by on the grass;
The fish in the fishpond
　　Gleam gold as they pass.

Superior tulips
　　Adorn the parterres
In the exquisite garden
　　Of Mr. Bellairs.

But ah, the great mansion,
　　The dark polished floors,
The marble, the mirrors,
　　The gilt on the doors,

The bedrooms so blissful,
  The bathrooms so roomy,
The books in the library
  All learned and gloomy,

The cherubs on ceilings
  And stags on the wall,
The family portraits
  That line the great hall,

The carpets, the curtains,
  The fat chintzy chairs—
Oh, what a palazzo
  Has Mr. Bellairs!

With such a great mansion
  And so many stairs
No wonder he's haughty
  And gives himself airs.

No wonder he's haughty
  With such an abode,
And his nose is quite straight
  Like the old Roman road.

Mrs. Golightly

Mrs. Golightly's goloshes
    Are roomy and large;
Through water she slithers and sloshes,
    As safe as a barge.

When others at home must be stopping,
    To market she goes,
And returns later on with her shopping
    Tucked into her toes.

Little Minnie Mystery

Little Minnie Mystery has packets and parcels
  All tied about with laces and strings,
And all full of scraps and patches and morsels
  And oddments and pieces and bits of things.

All tied about with strings and laces
  Are old Minnie Mystery's wonderful stores,
And she stows them away in all sorts of places—
  Cupboards and cases and chests of drawers.

All day long you will hear her caper
  From attic to basement, up and down stairs,
Rummaging and rustling with tissue paper
  And rattling keys and climbing on chairs.

What does she keep in her parcels and packets?—
  Why, buckles and beads and knobs and handles,
Playing-cards, curtain-rings, loops, and lockets,
  Letters and labels and Christmas-tree candles,

And a sea-shell box, and a peacock feather,
  And a picture postcard from Tonypandy—
Everything neat and fastened together,
  All that could possibly come in handy.

'Waste not, want not,' says Minnie Mystery.
  'Everything's sure to come in some day.'
So, although she should live till the end of history,
  Nothing she ever will throw away.

Mrs. Button

When Mrs. Button, of a morning,
  Comes creaking down the street,
You hear her old two black boots whisper
  'Poor feet—poor feet—poor feet!'

When Mrs. Button, every Monday,
  Sweeps the chapel neat,
All down the long, hushed aisles they whisper
  'Poor feet—poor feet—poor feet!'

Mrs. Button after dinner
  (It is her Sunday treat)
Sits down and takes her two black boots off
  And rests her two poor feet.

Mrs. Gilfillan

When Mrs. Gilfillan
  Is troubled with troubles,
She flies to the kitchen
  And sits blowing bubbles.
When Mrs. Gilfillan
  Is worried by money,
When her feet are like lead
  And her head's feeling funny,
When there's too much to do,
  And the chimney is smoking,
And everything's awkward
  And wrong and provoking,
When the washing won't dry
  For the rain's never ending,
When cupboards need cleaning
  And stockings want mending,
When the neighbours complain
  Of the noise of the cat,
And she ought to be looking
  For this and for that,
And never a line comes
  From her married daughter—
Then off to the kitchen
  With soap and warm water
Goes Mrs. Gilfillan
  And all of her troubles;
And she puffs them away
  In a great cloud of bubbles.
In joyful abandon
  She puffs them and blows them,

And all round about her
    In rapture she throws them;
When round, clear and shiny
    They hang in the air,
Away like a shadow
    Goes worry and care.

My Singing Aunt

The voice of magic melody
  With which my aunt delights me,
It drove my uncle to the grave
  And now his ghost affrights me.
This was the song she used to sing
  When I could scarcely prattle,
And as her top notes rose and fell
  They made the sideboard rattle:

'What makes a lady's cheeks so red,
  Her hair both long and wavy?
'Tis eating up her crusts of bread,
  Likewise her greens and gravy.
What makes the sailor tough and gay?
  What makes the ploughboy whistle?
'Tis eating salt-beef twice a day,
  And never mind the gristle.'

Thus sang my aunt in days gone by
  To soothe, caress, and calm me;
But what delighted me so much
  Drove her poor husband barmy.
So now when past the church I stray,
  'Tis not the night-wind moaning,
That chills my blood and stops my breath,
  But poor old uncle's groaning.

Diddling

The people of Diddling
Are never more than middling
For they can't abide either cold or heat.
If the weather is damp,
It gives them cramp,
And a touch of frost goes straight to their feet.

A thundery shower
Turns everything sour,
And a dry spell ruins the farmers' crops,
And a south-west wind
Is nobody's friend
For it blows the smoke down the chimney-tops.

Says old Mrs. Morley,
   'I'm middling poorly,
But thank you, I never was one to complain;
   For the cold in my nose
   As soon as it goes
I dursn't but say I may get it again.'

   Old Grandfather Snell
   Has never been well
Since he took to his crutches at seventy-three;
   And the elder Miss Lake
   Has a travelling ache
Which finds its way down from her neck to her knee.

   The people of Diddling
   Are never more than middling—
Not one but has headaches or palsy or gout.
   But what they fear worst
   Is a fine sunny burst,
For then there'll be nothing to grumble about.

Poor Rumble

Pity poor Rumble: he is growing wheezy.
  At seventy-nine years old
His breath comes hard, and nothing comes too easy.
  He finds the evenings cold.

Pity poor Rumble: winter on his noddle
  Has laid its wisps of snow;
And though about the place he scarce can toddle,
  He likes to work, I know.

Pity poor Rumble: his last teeth are rotting
  Back in his square old head;
And yet, come Whitsuntide, you'll find him potting
  Down in his potting-shed.

Pity poor Rumble: since the time of Noah
    There was in all the county
For rose, or root, or greens no better grower—
    It was sheer bounty.

He was the champion for fruit or tatey;
    But Rumble's famous marrow,
So huge it was and more than common weighty,
    It almost split his barrow.

Of cat and dog he was the holy terror—
    None ever plagued him twice;
And if a slug walked on his lawn in error,
    His language was not nice.

Pity poor Rumble: now his strength is going.
    No more he'll cut up wood.
I wish I had some peaches of his growing;
    They were so very good.

Sing, birds of the air, for Martin Rumble, please.
    When he is gone away,
Who will grow strawberries for you, green peas,
    And currants on the spray?

THE STREET

MUSICIAN

The Street Musician

(based on the words of a song by Schubert)

With plaintive fluting, sad and slow,
  The old man by the roadside stands.
Who would have thought such notes could flow
  From such cracked lips and withered hands?

On shivering legs he stoops and sways,
  And not a passer stops to hark;
No penny cheers him as he plays;
  About his feet the mongrels bark.

But piping through the bitter weather,
  He lets the world go on its way.
Old piper! let us go together,
  And I will sing and you shall play.

Fireworks

They rise like sudden fiery flowers
  That burst upon the night,
Then fall to earth in burning showers
  Of crimson, blue, and white.

Like buds too wonderful to name,
  Each miracle unfolds,
And catherine-wheels begin to flame
  Like whirling marigolds.

Rockets and Roman candles make
  An orchard of the sky,
Whence magic trees their petals shake
  Upon each gazing eye.

The Statue

On a stone chair in the market-place
Sits a stone gentleman with a stone face.
He is great, he is good, he is old as old—
How many years I've not been told.
Great things he did a great while ago,
And what they were I do not know.
But solemn and sad is his great square face
As he sits high up on his square stone base.
Day after day he sits just so,
With some words in a foreign tongue below.
Whether the wind blows warm or cold,
His stone clothes alter never a fold.
One stone hand he rests on his knee;
With the other stone hand he points at me.
Oh, why does he look at me in just that way?
I'm afraid to go, and afraid to stay:
Stone gentleman, what have you got to say?

The Piano

There is a lady who plays a piano;
  She lets me listen if I keep still.
I love to watch her twinkling fingers
  Fly up and down in scale or trill.

I love to hear the great chords crashing
  And making the huge black monster roar;
I love to hear the little chords falling
  Like sleepy waves on a summer shore.

Here comes an army with drums and trumpets,
  Now it's a battlefield, now it's a fire;
Now it's a waterfall boiling and bubbling,
  Now it's a bird singing higher and higher.

Now in the moonlight watch the trees bending,
  Water-nymphs rise from the bed of a stream;
Now in the garden the fountains are playing
  And in the sunshine flowers sway and dream.

Sometimes Harlequin comes with sweet Columbine,
  Sometimes I see deserts and twinkling stars,
The goose-girl, the fairies, a giant, a pygmy,
  And dark muffled strangers in foreign bazaars. . . .

All these I see when I hear that piano,
  All these and many things more do I see,
While over the keyboard the lady's hands travel,
  Yet nothing she sings, and no word says she.

Rum Lane

Gusty and chill
  Blows the wind in Rum Lane,
And the spouts are a-spill
  With the fast-driving rain.

No footfall, no sound!
  Not a cat slithers by.
Men of sense, I'll be bound,
  Are at home in the dry.

Tall, dark, and narrow
  Are houses and shops—
Scarce room for a sparrow
  Between the roof-tops.

But oh! what a history
  Of rum and romance
Could be made from the mystery
  Of old Rum Lane once—

For this was the place
  Where they stowed silk apparel,
Old wine and old lace,
  And rum in the barrel!

Gusty and chill
  Blows the wind in Rum Lane,
And the spouts are a-spill
  With the fast-driving rain.

But no footfall, no tread,
    No step on the cobble
Will fright you in bed,
    You can sleep free of trouble;

For smuggling is over,
    And never again
Will any wild rover
    Be caught in Rum Lane.

Uriconium

There was a man of Uriconium
Who played a primitive harmonium,
Inventing, to relieve his tedium,
Melodies high, low, and medium,
And standing on his Roman cranium
Amidst a bed of wild geranium,
Better known as pelargonium,
Since with odium his harmonium
Was received in Uriconium.

The Black Pebble

There went three children down to the shore,
    Down to the shore and back;
There was skipping Susan and bright-eyed Sam
    And little scowling Jack.

Susan found a white cockle-shell,
    The prettiest ever seen,
And Sam picked up a piece of glass
    Rounded and smooth and green.

But Jack found only a plain black pebble
    That lay by the rolling sea,
And that was all that ever he found;
    So back they went all three.

The cockle-shell they put on the table,
    The green glass on the shelf,
But the little black pebble that Jack had found,
    He kept it for himself.

Pat's Fiddle

When Pat plays his fiddle
  In the great empty hall,
And the flame of each candle
  Is shiny and small,
     Then to hear the brave jingle,
     Oh, how my feet tingle
And how I do wish we could have a fine ball!

     Like a riddle, like a riddle
      Without any answer,
     Is a fiddle, sweet fiddle,
      With never a dancer.

Then out of the shadows
  And down the dark stairs
Come the ghosts of bright ladies
  And tall cavaliers.
     Oh, see with what pleasure
     They step out the measure!
His heart is as gay as the colour she wears.

     Like a riddle, like a riddle
      Without any answer,
     Is a fiddle, sweet fiddle,
      With never a dancer.

I hear from each partner
  Who passes me by
The faintest of whispers,
  The ghost of a sigh.
     For there'll be no hiding
     The pain of dividing
When the strains of the fiddle shall falter and die.

Like a riddle, like a riddle
  Without any answer,
Is a fiddle, sweet fiddle,
  With never a dancer.

So play no more, Paddy,
  Of fiddlers the best.
The spent candles bid us
  Good-night and good rest.
    When music entrancing
    Sets both my feet dancing,
There's something inside me that can't be expressed.
    Now rest your old fingers
    While darkness yet lingers,
For yonder has vanished the last ghostly guest.

Boating

Gently the river bore us
  Beneath the morning sky,
Singing, singing, singing
Its reedy, quiet tune
  As we went floating by;
And all the afternoon
  In our small boat we lay
Rocking, rocking, rocking
  Under the willows grey.

When into bed that evening
   I climbed, it seemed a boat
Was softly rocking, rocking,
Rocking me to sleep,
   And I was still afloat.
I heard the grey leaves weep
   And whisper round my bed,
The river singing, singing,
   Singing through my head.

MYTHS AND

WONDERS

Giant Thunder

Giant Thunder, striding home,
Wonders if his supper's done.

'Hag wife, hag wife, bring me my bones!'
'They are not done,' the old hag moans.

'Not done? not done?' the giant roars
And heaves his old wife out of doors.

Cries he, 'I'll have them, cooked or not!'
But overturns the cooking-pot.

He flings the burning coals about;
See how the lightning flashes out!

Upon the gale the old hag rides,
The cloudy moon for terror hides.

All the world with thunder quakes;
Forest shudders, mountain shakes;
From the cloud the rainstorm breaks;
Village ponds are turned to lakes;
Every living creature wakes.

Hungry Giant, lie you still!
Stamp no more from hill to hill—
Tomorrow you shall have your fill.

The Magic Seeds

There was an old woman who sowed a corn seed,
And from it there sprouted a tall yellow weed.
She planted the seeds of the tall yellow flower,
And up sprang a blue one in less than an hour.
The seed of the blue one she sowed in a bed,
And up sprang a tall tree with blossoms of red.
And high in the treetop there sang a white bird,
And his song was the sweetest that ever was heard.
The people they came from far and from near,
The song of the little white bird for to hear.

Pluto and Proserpine

Said Pluto the King
   To Princess Proserpine,
'I will give you a marriage ring
   If you will be my Queen.'

Said she, 'What flowers spring
   Underneath your sun?'
Said he, 'Where I am King
   Flowers there are none.'

'And do the gay birds sing
   In your country?' said she,
'You shall hear where I am King
   None but the owl,' said he.

'Do the people laugh and play?'
   Asked Princess Proserpine.
'Are the children happy as day
   In the meadows soft and green?'

Said the King, 'There are no meadows
   In the country where I reign.
My people are all shadows;
   They will not laugh again.

'Sunshine you shall not see
   In the Kingdom of the Dead:
Queen of that kingdom you shall be,
   If you and I are wed.'

Said she, 'I am tired of flowers
  And the gay birds' song;
I am tired of the sunny hours
  In the meadows day long.

'But the dark I will not fear,
  And you and I will wed;
And the sad ones I will cheer
  In the grey land of the dead.'

So Pluto the King
  Took the Princess by the hand,
And with the marriage ring
  Made her Queen in his land.

Troy

Priam is the king of ashes.
   Heroes die and gods lament.
Round his head his kingdom crashes.
   Now the ten years' war is spent.

Night in flames and no man sleeping,
   Trumpets' scream across the plains,
Charging horsemen, women weeping—
   These are all that now remains:

These and not the shouts of gladness,
   Not the victors' face of joy,
These I see and hear in sadness
   When I think of fallen Troy.

The Moonlit Stream

A stream far off beneath the moon
  Flowed silver-bright and thin,
Winding its way like some slow tune
  Played on a violin.

The valley trees were hushed and still;
  The sky was pearly grey;
The moonlight slept upon the hill—
  As white as snow it lay.

Then softly from a ruined tower
  That rose beside the stream
A bell chimed out the midnight hour;
  And then—Oh, did I dream?—

Then all at once a long, black boat
    With neither sail nor oars
Down that bright stream began to float
    Between its shadowy shores.

No passenger nor steersman stirred
    On that enchanted thing;
But faint, unearthly-sweet, I heard
    A choir of voices sing.

It moved mysterious and serene,
    A sable-feathered swan;
It seemed the soul of some sad queen
    Was borne to Avalon.

So in my thoughts that shadowy boat
    Will sail the moonlit river,
And faintly I shall hear the note
    Of that sad choir for ever.

Bobadil

Far from far
  Lives Bobadil
In a tall house
  On a tall hill.

Out from the high
  Top window-sill
On a clear night
  Leans Bobadil

To touch the moon,
  To catch a star,
To keep in her tall house
  Far from far.

The Three Singing Birds

The King walked in his garden green,
  Where grew a marvellous tree;
And out of its leaves came singing birds
  By one, and two, and three.

The first bird had wings of white,
  The second had wings of gold,
The third had wings of deepest blue
  Most beauteous to behold.

The white bird flew to the northern land,
  The gold bird flew to the west,
The blue bird flew to the cold, cold south
  Where never bird might nest.

The King waited a twelvemonth long,
  Till back the three birds flew,
They lighted down upon the tree,
  The white, the gold, and the blue.

The white bird brought a pearly seed
  And gave it to the King;
The gold bird from out of the west
  He brought a golden ring.

The third bird with feathers blue
  Who came from the far cold south,
A twisted sea-shell smooth and grey
  He carried in his mouth.

The King planted the pearly seed
  Down in his garden green,
And up there sprang a pearl-white maid,
  The fairest ever seen.

She looked at the King and knelt her down
  All under the magic tree,
She smiled at him with her red lips
  But not a word said she.

Instead she took the grey sea-shell
  And held it to his ear,
She pressed it close and soon the King
  A strange, sweet song did hear.

He raised the fair maid by the hand
  Until she stood at his side;
Then he gave her the golden ring
  And took her for his bride.

And at their window sang the birds,
    They sang the whole night through,
Then off they went at break of day,
    The white, the gold, and the blue.

Kingdom Cove

When I went down to Kingdom Cove,
The cliffs were brown, the sea was mauve.
Shadows of rocks on the clifftops lay
As the sunset flamed across the bay.
I saw three starfish upon the shore
And up in the sky was one fish more.
Birds on the tumbling waters cried
'Ship's away with the morning tide!'
But the man in the lighthouse called to me,
'Don't go crossing the tumbling sea!'
And I saw his telescope up to his eye
Gazing out to the sunset sky.
So I shouted out, 'But the night is black:
If I don't go on, I can't go back!'
And then a great storm cracked the sky
And a giant sea-bird scouted by,
He carried me off on his cloudy track
And set me down on a dolphin's back.
There is an island out to sea,
Where tall trees wait to sing for me;
Sing they will in the autumn gale,
And there on the dolphin's back I'll sail.
In Kingdom Cove my father stands,
Shading his eyes with two brown hands,
And three red starfish crumble away
And the land-breeze blows them across the bay.

The Horn

'Oh, hear you a horn, mother, behind the hill?
My body's blood runs bitter and chill.
The seven long years have passed, mother, passed,
And here comes my rider at last, at last.
I hear his horse now, and soon I must go.
How dark is the night, mother, cold the winds blow.
How fierce the hurricane over the deep sea!
For a seven years' promise he comes to take me.'

'Stay at home, daughter, stay here and hide.
I will say you have gone, I will tell him you died.
I am lonely without you, your father is old;
Warm is our hearth, daughter, but the world is cold.'

'Oh mother, Oh mother, you must not talk so.
In faith I promised, and for faith I must go,
For if that old promise I should not keep,
For seven long years, mother, I would not sleep.

Seven years my blood would run bitter and chill
To hear that sad horn, mother, behind the hill.
My body once frozen by such a shame
Would never be warmed, mother, at your hearth's flame.
But round my true heart shall the arms of the storm
For ever be folded, protecting and warm.'

TIME TO GO

HOME

Time to Go Home

Time to go home!
　Says the great steeple clock.
Time to go home!
　Says the gold weathercock.
Down sinks the sun
　In the valley to sleep;
Lost are the orchards
　In blue shadows deep.
Soft falls the dew
　On cornfield and grass;
Through the dark trees
　The evening airs pass:
Time to go home,
　They murmur and say;
Birds to their homes
　Have all flown away.
Nothing shines now
　But the gold weathercock.
Time to go home!
　Says the great steeple clock.

REPRINTED LITHOGRAPHICALLY IN GREAT BRITAIN
AT THE UNIVERSITY PRESS, OXFORD
BY VIVIAN RIDLER
PRINTER TO THE UNIVERSITY